Bull City Ghosts
Haunts of Durham

By William Jackson

This book is dedicated to the many generations of my family that have lived and worked in Durham for over 130 years.

Disclaimer:

While all attempts have been made to verify the information provided in this publication, neither the author nor the publisher assumes any responsibility for errors, omissions, or contrary interpretations of the subject matter herein.

This book is for entertainment purposes only. The views expressed are those of the author alone, and should not be taken as expert instruction or commands. The reader is responsible for his or her own actions.

Neither the author nor the publisher assumes any responsibility or liability whatsoever on the behalf of the purchaser or reader of these materials.

Any perceived slight of any individual or organization is purely unintentional.

Acknowledgments

I would like to thank my wife Michelle who has always been a driving force behind these writings, and to my daughters Anna, Lauren, Chloe and Mackenzie, who have always been supportive and forgiving of the time that I have spent researching and writing. I would also like to thank my brother Rick Jackson who has been instrumental in getting this work published, without their collective support throughout the years this endeavor would have been impossible.

Table of Contents

Introduction

My interest in ghosts and the paranormal has spanned my entire life. I remember as a young boy listening to the tales told by the elderly members of the family. Some of those tales are included in this book and my other book, "Ghosts of the Triangle, Historic Haunts of Raleigh, Durham, and Chapel Hill." There was nothing better than sitting wide-eyed on a late summer evening listening to these tales unwind, then running home in the dark and hiding under the covers. Hearing the chirping crickets through the screen door, I was sure that they were the sounds of some ethereal being coming to get me.

These stories gave me an appreciation for our family's history, Durham's history, and our state's history. Once I started school, it led me to scour the library for other tales of North Carolina's haunted past. Books by great authors such as Nancy Roberts, John Harden, Fred T. Morgan, Catherine Carter, and of course, Judge Charles Harry Whedbee fired my interest for years. Not only were they an exciting read, but for me, they brought the past alive.

My reasoning for writing these books is to continue in that tradition. In the age of video games, computers, and hundreds of cable television channels, my goal is for youngsters to pick up a book and read it. I want to hopefully rekindle an appreciation for our past, old folk tales, and legends that are an integral part of our history as a people.

As I write this book, my greatest desire is to pass Durham's history and folklore onto our next generation. If this book sparks an interest in just a handful of people, then I will have accomplished what I have set out to do.

History of Durham

Doctor Bartlett Durham

Although the town was founded in 1869 and the county in 1881, Durham had its official beginnings in the 1850s when Dr. Bartlett Durham gifted land to establish a railroad station. From then on, the town was known as Durham's Station and later Durham. But the history of the land goes back even further. The area that would become Durham had witnessed centuries of history.

The earliest inhabitants were hunter-gatherers and arrived in the area as early as 12,000

BCE. These native peoples gathered from the abundant woods and harvested game such as deer, elk, bear, and bison. These first people eventually laid down roots and took up agriculture, settling into permanent villages. A similar example of one of these villages can be found today in Hillsborough, NC, a few miles from Durham.

One of the first non-native men to document his visit to the region was John Lederer, who was commissioned by William Berkeley, the Royal Governor of the colony of Virginia. He explored the area's backcountry and wrote about it in The Discoveries of John Lederer In three several marches from Virginia to the West of Carolina, And Other parts of the Continent, began March 1669 and ended in September 1670.

The next Englishman to move about and record his travels to what is now modern-day Durham was John Lawson in 1701. Lawson recounts traveling through the area and stopping at a native town called Adshusheer, which is believed to be in the New Hope Creek area near Durham. Lawson recorded his travels in A New Voyage to Carolina.

After the visitation by these two explorers 30 years apart, the area would not see an influx of European settlement of any size until after 1750. Most of these settlements took place along the northeast of the county on crown land grants from the Earl of Granville. Some of these early prominent settlers were William Johnston of Snow

Hill Plantation, Richard Bennehan of Stagville, and William Clenny of Hardscrabble Plantation. The settlement would eventually spread out amongst the Little, Flat, and Eno Rivers' river valleys. A thriving settlement emerged on the Eno known as West Point, and more settlers were drawn to the region after the American Revolution.

The population steadily grew with the dawning of the nineteenth century. The more extensive plantations continued to prosper, and a steady stream of yeoman farmers dotted the landscape. Several new settlements began popping up south of the earlier communities nearer to the modern-day downtown Durham area. A community known as Pinhook developed to the west, and Prattsburg grew to the east.

In 1853, the rail station was established on four acres of land donated by Dr. Bartlett Durham, hence the name Durham Station. By the end of the Civil War in 1865, which effectively occurred just a few miles west of the station at James Bennet's Farm on the Hillsborough Road, Durham's future was sealed. The high demand for the bright leaf tobacco that Union and Confederate forces had become unaccustomed to while in the area led to Durham's post-war tobacco boom. John Green's Bull Durham Tobacco was in high demand, and in 1869 Green partnered with William Blackwell, who, after Green's death, bought out the company and partnered with Julian Carr and James Day and began cornering the market in the tobacco industry.

By far, the most dynamic family to prosper from the industry was the Duke family. The Duke family would become the most dominant force in post-war Durham, contributing to the tobacco, cotton, and other textile industries. The philanthropic Dukes would also provide hefty endowments for hospitals, orphanages, and schools, most notably Trinity College, which would later become Duke University.

Post-Civil War Durham also provided many opportunities for African Americans unavailable in most other parts of the south. By the beginning of the 20th century, Durham was home to the National Religious Training School at Chautauqua, modern-day NC Central University, Lincoln Hospital, and the North Carolina Mutual Life Insurance Company. The latter became the largest black-owned financial institute and the centerpiece of Parrish Street in downtown, which would be known nationwide as "Black Wall Street."

The first half of the 20th century saw the continued boom of the textiles, tobacco, cotton, and hosiery mills. These mills operated around the clock running 24 hours a day to keep up with their products' high demand. The century was so lucrative that even two world wars and a great depression could not slow the economy of this town that was less than 100 years old.

The last half of the 20th century saw many changes come to Durham. The formation of the Research Triangle Park and the textile industries' gradual closing ushered in a new era for the city. By the 1980s, Durham was transitioning from textiles and tobacco to research and development. The old factories were closed, and many sat vacant through the '80s and '90s.

The dawn of the 21st century has seen a revival in Durham. Once empty, tobacco warehouses and cotton mills now house small businesses, craft breweries, artistic communities, and living spaces. New apartment complexes dot, and in some instances rise above, the skyline. Though it's different, not everything changes. The Durham Bulls still play baseball on spring and summer evenings, and downtown has seen a resurgent nightlife once again. Through all the years, Durham has been and will remain the home of a unique group of people - proud of their past, looking toward the future, and proud to be from the Bull City.

Comfort in the Storm

During the early 1960s, a young girl in Durham was terribly frightened of the summer thunderstorms. Every time a summer storm would pass by, the girl would always run to the arms of her grandpa, who also had a terrible fear of the storms, to weather it out in his lap with his big arms tight around her. He would always tell her not to worry that he would protect her and not let anything happen to her. No matter how severe the storm was, she always felt safe and comfortable under his protection. No matter how frightened he was, he was always strong for his little granddaughter's sake.

Years went by, and the grandpa eventually passed away, leaving the granddaughter to go through the summer storms alone. No matter how old she got, she always remembered the comforting feeling of being with her grandpa and how it would ease her fears. She learned later that he was terrified of the storms, which made her feel even closer to him than she did before. She never knew that although he was afraid, he put his fear aside to comfort her. So, long after her grandpa was gone, she would be able to get through the nights of rain pelting the windows, the low rumblings of thunder, and flashes of lightning by knowing that he had put his fear aside for her. She always felt that her grandpa was watching over her, and it comforted her.

One particular rainy evening in the mid-1980s, she left work looking up at the dark sky, making it seem much later than it really was. She walked to her car, fumbling, trying to get her keys out of her purse to open up her door. At the same time, she maintained control of her umbrella to protect herself against the driving rain. Soaking wet, she slid into the driver's seat and started the car. By now, the thunder was crashing overhead, and lightning flashed across the sky, creating eerie shadows along the wet city streets. As many storms as she had weathered since the passing of her grandfather, this was by far the worst, and no matter how much she tried, she just couldn't as she had in the past feel her grandpa's presence and comfort. She drove slowly with both hands on the steering wheel, trying her best to navigate the dark streets, straining to see through the windshield.

Suddenly a loud crash of thunder burst overhead, completely frightening the woman, almost causing her to lose control and run off the road. In tears, she felt so alone and scared until something caught her eye. It was movement coming from the back seat of her car. Quickly she adjusted her mirror, and there, staring at her was her grandpa. He sat there silently and looked back at her with a smile on his face. She knew that he was there to tell her that everything was alright and that he was there to protect her as he had been so many times before. In the blink of an eye, he was gone, but she could still feel his presence as she had so many times in the past. Comforted as if she were a child, she continued home with all the confidence and assurance of one who had conquered their fears.

She never tried to explain what occurred that night, not to others or to herself as she told the story. She didn't know if it was her grandfather's spirit who had come to comfort her in a time of need or if it was her mind seeing something that she so desperately needed at that moment. Either way, it was a vision of a dearly departed loved one who, when needed, was there as he had been so many times and so many years before.

North Carolina School of Science and Mathematics

Watts Hospital circa 1914

Set amongst ancient oaks and well-manicured lawns sits the NC School of Science and Mathematics (NCSSM). Opened in 1980 with 150 high school students, it is a unique public residential high school specializing in science and mathematics that draws talented students from all reaches of North Carolina. The school is housed in a beautiful Italianate structure that was originally Watts Hospital. Watts opened its doors in 1909 and served Durham's citizens until 1976 when Lincoln and Watts formed Durham County General Hospital. Since Watts Hospital closed and NCSSM took over the campus, there have been many tales of unexplained events that have taken place reported by students, staff, and the occasional visitor to campus.

One such story was told by a long-time maintenance worker working underneath a particular portion of the old hospital one day. He was distracted when he heard the unmistakable voice say, "Give me my medicine." He stopped working, unsure if his mind was playing tricks on him. He slowly turned around and saw what he described as a figure of what appeared to be an elderly male in a hospital gown laying on his side. The worker beat a hasty retreat from under the building. He was never able to explain why an apparition would appear to him under the hospital. Still, from that day forward until he retired, he refused to work under the building under any circumstances.

Another employee, a security officer, was working late one night during the summer. The students and staff were out on summer vacation, and the buildings on campus were all empty and silent. He stood in the hall of one of those buildings reading a bulletin board, trying to pass the time when he heard the unmistakable ring of the elevator by the cafeteria as if someone had summoned it on an upper floor.

He paid little attention as this was a common occurrence in the old building for the elevators to open and close independently. Still, on this particular night, the doors on the upper floor closed, and the elevator moaned and groaned, making its way down to the dark first-floor lobby. Still reading the bulletin board and only half paying attention to the noise behind him, the officer noticed the elevator doors began to open, and light flooded into the dark lobby and illuminated the elevator's inside on the reflective glass of the bulletin board. His attention was immediately drawn to the light, and in the reflection, he noticed a man standing inside with his arm resting on the elevator's wall. He wore a plaid shirt and had dark curly hair with a thick mustache. The security guard was caught off guard when the man's reflection made eye contact with him and smiled as the doors began to close.

"Wait," the security officer thought, "No one should be inside this building."

He spun around just as the door closed and hit the button to open the elevator doors immediately. To his surprise and amazement, as the doors opened and light once again flooded into the lobby, he was staring into an empty elevator. It occurred to him that the gentleman's reflection that he had seen looked as if he had just stepped out of the 1970s, and perhaps he had.

Another young man shared an interesting story that happened years ago when he was a teenager. It had been a quiet night; boredom seemed to prevail with the young man as he sat watching his father work. His father, a security officer, had recently taken the job not long after the transition from the hospital to the school, so the young man thought it would be interesting to accompany his father to work and explore some old buildings.

"Time to make a round," which meant they were going to walk through the building and around the campus to check all of the doors and windows to make sure everything was secure. He excitedly got up and hurriedly moved to the security office door.

He was thankful to get up and move around and leave the confines of the tiny security office. He was fascinated by the thoughts of how many people had been born, died, and suffered there. The great emotions that this building had seen over the years had to be immense. His father explained to him that where they were at was what used to be the old hallway leading to the morgue. It was dark, really dark; the only windows were little, small panes high up from the floor. It was almost like being inside of a tunnel. In the pitch-black night, the rain had begun to fall and was pelting those small panes running down in little rivulets to the sash illuminated periodically by flashes of lightning that would cast an eerie glow to the inside of the tunnel creating odd shadows along the wall.

The young boy heard the click of the door as his father locked it behind them. They crept down to the other end of the hallway. Something feeling not exactly right contributed to the silence between them. The wind began to pick up, and the rain and lightning increased as the summer storm intensified outside. Just as the two reached the other end of the hallway, a loud hideous cackle erupted directly behind the two of them, a laugh so hideous and evil it caused every hair on the boy's body to stand on end, and he saw a look on his father's face he would never forget.

His dad scrambled and fumbled with the keys and was finally able to unlock the door, and both ran through. Safely on the other side, the boy asked his dad what that noise was, and his father said,

"I don't know, son, but I hear things like that all of the time."

The boy never forgot that night and that evil laugh. All he knows is that it happened and that there was no way that anyone could have been in that locked hallway with only one way in and one way out. Well, at least no one from our physical world.

Typical of these events, many others have reported similar events over the years - disembodied voices, spectral footsteps, and full-bodied apparitions. There are even claims that the sound of a creaking old wheelchair can be heard making its way down one of the corridors. Interestingly, reports from one resident franticly told of an old lady in a nightgown calling for help in the bathroom near what used to be the old emergency room of the hospital. Security was notified, and they discovered no one in the bathroom, the campus was locked down, and a search was conducted over the grounds to no avail. There was no elderly lady in a nightgown on campus, nor should there have been. Could this have been an apparition from days gone by? Strangely enough, in the same restroom area, the ghost of a man has been reported entering the men's bathroom. Individuals in the bathroom stalls report the bathroom door opening and a man with gray pants and black dress shoes walking in. The man will walk out of sight but never leaves. There are many reports of looking for the individual that came in but never left, but he has never been found.

So many stories come from the halls of these old buildings. So many people throughout the years have had their lives permanently changed within those walls. The loss of loved ones, sickness, and births have all occurred here. So much energy has been left behind that it appears to be played repeatedly as if on a continuous loop, never ceasing. Maybe one day, these restless spirits will find peace and be able to move on. Until then, they will continue to make their presence known to those around them.

North Carolina School of Science and Mathematics today

The Spinsters Ghost

Traveling down the 3800 Block of Chapel Hill Road, one would not immediately ponder the existence of ghosts or spirits roaming in this urban residential area teeming with single-family homes and apartment buildings, but looks can be deceiving. Such is the case with one such home in the area, which is vacant once again at the time of this book's writing as it has been so many times since the death of its owner.

The house is a small gray, unimposing structure built in the 1920s by Dr. Cox, who conducted his practice out of the home for several years before his death. After the passing of Dr. Cox, his spinster sister Ms. Lindsey remained in the house until she died in 1977, at which time mysterious things began to transpire in and around the old home.

Dean, a neighbor who has lived next door since the early 1980s, had his first encounter with Ms. Lindsey days after moving in. One afternoon, he was outside in his house's back yard doing some work when his attention was drawn to the window of what he thought was an empty house. As he stared at the window, he could see the figure of an elderly female with her hair pulled back on her head wearing an old-fashioned dress staring back at him. Shaken a bit, he looked away momentarily only to find her gone when he looked back to the window.

Believing the home to be vacant, Dean approached the owner the next time he saw him checking on the property.

"Who is living in the house now," he asked the owner.

"No one," the owner replied.

When Dean proceeded to describe what he had seen, he was told he had seen the ghost of Ms. Lindsey. Although she had died five years before Dean had moved next door, and he had never laid eyes on her, he was able to describe her in detail to the homeowner. The relationship he forged with the owner led to his becoming a caretaker for the residence. It was in this role that he had many more experiences in and around the home.

One of those experiences Dean described was an encounter he had while checking on something in the basement. As he was working, he noticed the floor joists overhead creaking as if under some weight, like someone was upstairs walking. He then heard muffled talking and the sound as if someone upstairs had turned on a radio playing music from a bygone era. Thinking maybe someone had broken in or that some local kids were hanging out in the abandoned residence, Dean raced upstairs to find out what was going on. Once upstairs, he found absolutely nothing, just an old vacant house and a quietness that was almost too quiet; he described it as an uneasy stillness.

During one of the renovation periods, it was decided to remove the old piano in the house. On several occasions, Dean would hear beautiful music coming from the piano, but once he approached it, the music would stop. Even after the old piano had deteriorated, musical strains could still be heard emitting from the dilapidated remains. This is also the period in its vacancy when a woman fitting the description of Ms. Lindsey could be seen standing along the house's back railing. Several different people reported this on other occasions.

When the renovations were over, and the house was finally rented out, new tenants complained of hearing walking and talking throughout the night. One renter even reported hearing ghostly piano tunes at 2 AM every morning, even though the piano's rotted remains had been hauled away before anyone moved in. Most of the tenants never remained long.

Dean remembers one of them approaching him in his front yard one day and told him that he had not been able to sleep in his bed since he had moved into the home. Every night noises and disturbances in his bedroom would prompt him to get up and spend what was left of the night sleeping fitfully in the bathtub, the only place that he would not be bothered. When Dean found out what room he was sleeping in, he told him to switch rooms. The room that he had been trying to occupy was Ms. Lindsey's room. As soon as he switched bedrooms, he had no more problems and lived peacefully in the house for a couple of years before leaving.

According to Dean, the last family to rent the house had a small girl. They spent several months in the house, and Dean spoke to the father regularly. The family never did admit to seeing or hearing anything the entire time they lived there. Strangely, as the moving trucks were there and the last of their belongings had been loaded, the father walked over and shook Dean's hand to tell him goodbye. He looked at him with an uncomfortable look on his face and said to him that the night before, the last night they would spend in the home, they were awakened by the cries of their young daughter. When they got to her bedroom, she was sitting up in bed and told them that a little older woman had been in her bedroom and had frightened her. The father did not know how to explain it, and he did not want to. He told Dean he was just glad they were leaving.

About two weeks after they had left and the home was unoccupied once again, Dean was standing in the back yard enjoying the pleasant weather of the late spring twilight. He noticed something in the backyard of the house. It was a mist, and suddenly the fog began to take shape, the shape of a human body, and once the human shape had been completely formed, the misty figure slowly began to float up, and it disappeared into the late evening sky. That was the last mysterious occurrence Dean has seen in a long time, and he wonders if it was Ms. Lindsey's spirit finally moving on.

Interestingly, the experiences of events and happenings at this home all match up with stories told by everyone that ever reported an encounter spanning many decades. Dean has met tenants of all ages and walks of life, and each one of them associated with the house has had at least one strange encounter whether they lived there two years or two months. One thing common is that no one has ever been harmed. Dean thinks that there is nothing malicious or menacing about her spirit. He believes that she wants people to know that she is still around, although he is not sure after his last encounter. Still, he likes to think that she hasn't left just yet and whenever he leaves after checking on the home, he always walks to the door and says, "Good evening, Ms. Lindsey," as he turns out the light and locks the door behind him.

Specters at the Old Courthouse

Since its formation, Durham County has had four courthouses. The first is a red brick structure near the intersection of Main and Church Street completed in 1889. The second is a beautiful neoclassical structure built in 1916 on the same site as the original and is still being used to house county offices and the commissioner's chambers. The third structure, built in 1978, served as the Durham County Judicial Building until completing the new Justice Center on South Dillard Street in 2013.

The original Durham County Courthouse

The third courthouse appears to have been haunted almost from the moment it opened its doors. Built on the old Malbourne Hotel site, reports of strange happenings sprang up immediately by individuals who worked in the building. Those reports would significantly increase after an inmate hung himself. The jailers would describe mysterious occurrences that would take place on the 7th-floor detention center. Many were frightened by noises and disembodied voices coming from empty cells. The activity continued until the new detention building was constructed in the mid-1990s. All detention staff and inmates were moved to the new structure a couple of blocks south after its completion.

Once the inmates were removed, the vacant 7th floor was utilized for housing stacks of files for the clerk's office in the once overcrowded cells. Many were the timid clerk that had to make their way to the dreaded 7th floor to pull an old file for review. On one occasion, a deputy escorted a maintenance employee up to the old 7th-floor jail. The maintenance man made it clear that he did not like going up there alone. He said it felt as if someone was always watching or following you down the passageways. As the two men walked down the hall talking, the deputy dismissed any notions that the place was haunted. A large screw thrown from an unseen hand struck the deputy on the shoulder at that very instance. Both men heard the screw hit the floor, and as the deputy reached down to pick it up, he noticed the maintenance man running for the elevator. The deputy soon followed quickly with a newfound respect for whatever was lurking there.

In 2013, when the courthouse moved, maintenance employees were very wary of going into the abandoned courthouse. It seemed that now the old clerk's office on the 3rd floor had become just as active as the old 7th-floor jail. Reports of typing from phantom typewriters could be heard echoing through the rooms, and the distinct boom of the file stamp machine could be heard going off at random even though none of this equipment remained in the offices. Strange and disembodied voices could sometimes be heard, sometimes in a whisper, sometimes in a regular tone. There were many reports of footsteps walking through the hallways and offices of vacant floors.

Over the years, so much activity has taken place - people working, getting married, and just the county's daily business. Emotional scenarios played out within the building as it served the citizens of Durham. Those walls have seen distraught family members seeking justice for a murdered relative and those witnessing their loved ones being condemned to death. There is no wonder that such energy has imprinted itself at this location.

In 2016, the building was reconfigured inside and out and now houses beautiful new county offices that bear little resemblance to the old structure. Interestingly, one wonders if those ancient spirits still roam the new hallways today or if they are lost in the new maze of glass partitions that leave the new occupants a quiet workplace to enjoy.

The second Durham County Courthouse built in 1916

The third Durham County Courthouse built in 1978

The Black Mass

To see the house located on Ardesely Drive, "haunted" is probably not the first word that would come to mind. The house is an ordinary home by all accounts, a neat and trim brick ranch home typical of the late '60s and early 70's when this particular house was built. There is also nothing extraordinary about the home or land where it was made, for that matter, just woods and old farmland sitting in the county's eastern part. As a matter of fact, the home has seen only one owner throughout its almost 50-year existence. Nothing in the house's history would justify the experiences that a young boy would endure as he grew up there.

The first encounter the boy had was in the mid-1980s. One night, while watching television in his room, he saw something moving out of the corner of his eye. He watched, mesmerized as a dark black mass slowly moved across his bedroom disappearing into the wall on the other side of the room. His trance was suddenly interrupted by his mother's screams. He then realized that his mother and father's bedroom was on the other side of the wall where the black mass had entered. He ran to her and found her sitting up on the bed with a look of terror on her face. He asked her what was wrong, and she tried to act as if nothing had happened. She tried to keep from frightening him or his sister, who had also come in from her room. She told them that she had just seen a bug and that everything was ok. When his sister left to go back to her room, the boy told his mother that he knew what she had been screaming about. She tried to assure him that it was just a little bug running across the floor until he began to describe to her what he had seen float across his room and through the wall. She looked at him very seriously and began to tell him what had happened to her.

She explained that she had also been watching television when the screen began to jump and became fuzzy. Just as she was about to get up and check the television to see what was wrong, she noticed movement beside her bed. Coming through the wall was a black mass moving very slowly toward her bed. It came right up beside her, just floating in mid-air. Once she began screaming, it suddenly disappeared, and that's when they had entered her room. She told her son it would be best if they did not tell any of the rest of the family of their experiences to keep from frightening them. She assured her son that it was nothing to be afraid of and that there was a logical explanation for what had happened.

Although somewhat comforted by his mother's words, the young man could not get the image out of his mind. Many sleepless nights were spent in that room waiting for the hideous black mass to return. Though he waited, things seemed to calm down, and after a couple of weeks, he had almost forgotten about the incident. Thinking that maybe his mother had been right and there was, after all, a logical, natural explanation for the occurrence.

Several months passed, and life was as normal in the home as it had always been. Things were quiet, and it seemed as if it had never even happened; that's when the noises began. One night the boy was awakened out of a deep sleep by someone in his bathroom moving around. At first, he thought it was his sister up using the bathroom, but no light was on, and no one came out. He got up to investigate, only to find it unoccupied. He went back to sleep, thinking that he was just hearing things, but the noises continued. Night after night, he listened to the spectral sounds moving about in the bathroom, footsteps, water turning off and on, and cabinets opening and closing. He finally went to his mother, who told him that he was only imagining things and shouldn't let his mind play tricks on him.

Even though the noises continued, he had not had another visitation from whatever it was in their house until one night while watching television in the family room. It was late on a school night, and he had slipped into the family room to watch TV. Around 11 o'clock, he was all of a sudden overtaken with a sense of fear and dread. Something was drawing his eyes over to the doorway. He did not want to look because he knew what was there, but he couldn't stop himself. As he turned around, he was staring directly into the grotesque black mass hovering in the doorway. He couldn't move; he couldn't scream; it was as if he was temporarily paralyzed. The only thing he could do was stare at the mysterious being. He later recalled that he could sense pure evil emanating from the blob of inky blackness. As he watched in horror, the thing began to dissipate and then was gone. He quickly ran to his room and got ready for bed, sleeping that night with the lights on.

He was at a point that he didn't know what to do or who to turn to. His mom was now in denial of what happened even though she had seen it herself. He knew his father wouldn't believe him, and he didn't want to frighten his sister. He realized that it was something that he would just have to deal with on his own. He made it a point to never be in the house alone, and he always went to bed before the rest of the family went to bed.

The noises in his bathroom continued and actually intensified. Looking back, he felt as if it had been feeding off of his fear; the more scared he was, the more active it became. Things eventually spiraled out of control when one night, as he was lying in bed, he was physically assaulted by the entity. It had been a particularly restless night for the young boy, and he was lying on his back staring up at the ceiling of his bedroom. Out of nowhere, something grabbed the front of his t-shirt, and he began levitating off the bed as if something was picking him up by his shirt. He estimates that he was lifted about six inches off of his bed when that night, anger and frustration overcame fear. As he was being lifted, he began to shout at the unseen force to leave him alone and depart. He called on the name of God and was dropped back to his bed. He lifted himself up and continued to scream for the being to leave and never return.

He said that night it was as if a weight had been lifted off of him. He felt that he had been liberated from the clutches of this evil being. After that night, he never had any more contact with whatever evil force was present in the house. He believes that the entity was demonic to this day. Although he no longer lives in the house, it is still inhabited by his father. The latter has never complained of any strange occurrences over the years. It just proves that not all haunted houses have to be old or the site of tragic happenings. As the young boy, now a middle-aged man, who endured several years of terror can attest to. A haunting evil presence could manifest at any time to anyone anywhere.

Girl in Distress

It was a cloudy, dreary night. It had been a frigid winter, and the weatherman was calling for snow overnight. It wasn't snowing yet as the man went around checking his doors, ensuring that everything was locked up for the evening. His wife was already upstairs fast asleep, but he had felt the need to tie up a few loose ends leftover from work that day.

The couple lived in the northern part of the county in the Treyburn subdivision. It was usually quiet with nothing much out of the ordinary that took place. But this night would be different. Something would happen that they, although well-educated and intelligent, would never find a genuinely logical explanation for.

As the man checked the back door, he turned out the light and made his way up the staircase to his bedroom. About halfway up, he heard ever so low what sounded like a knock. He turned and went back downstairs to the front door. He looked out but didn't see anything but the lonely street illuminated by the orangish glow of the street light. Just as he was about to open the door, it came again, Knock, Knock, Knock, Knock! This time much louder and coming from the back door. His wife, awakened by the commotion, was now standing against the rail at the top of the steps.

"Who is it?" she asked. "I don't know. Go back to bed," he told her. He made his way now to the back door as a sense of uneasiness enveloped him. "Who would come to the back door at this time of night," he thought, mumbling it under his breath. He looked out the window and saw a young girl. The girl was in her late teens or early 20's, and though she was not poorly dressed, she appeared a bit disheveled and, if anything, a bit underdressed for the bitter cold outside. She seemed to have nothing on except a lightweight jacket, and her dark hair fell in strings around her pale face.

As he turned on the back porch light, he noticed how much paler she looked. Her clothes, now illuminated, looked more threadbare than they had when he peered through the window at her in the darkness. A few flurries had begun to fall and swirl in the frigid air as she looked up at him with an unnerving vacant stare. Her eyes seemed to set back and hollow to him, and her voice seemed monotone and expressionless as she asked, "May I use your phone? I need help."

Not about to let her inside after hearing about how people would use this tactic to rob unsuspecting homeowners, he told her to wait there. He closed the door, went to the hall table, picked up his cordless phone, and walked back to the door, but the girl was not there. As he scanned the backyard, he saw her as she disappeared into the woods behind his home. Oddly, it wasn't as if she were walking or running from his house. It was as if she was floating backwards, vanishing into the thick woods.

"That was odd," his wife said as she was now downstairs by his side. "Yes, it was very odd," he replied as he dialed 911 to report what had just happened. He knew he had to report it in case the girl was really in some type of trouble.

It only took about five minutes for the officer to arrive. He was a young, friendly man; the two stood in the front vestibule of his home as he began to explain what had transpired that night. Just as he was relating his story to the officer, his radio began to crackle. He listened as another call came across the waves, "young girl, possibly in distress knocking on the door, has now left the scene..." The address given was just three houses down from his own. Another officer answered up that he was in the area and would check on that call. As the man began to talk to the officer again, they were interrupted by his radio once more. "Report of young girl knocking on door, possibly in distress..." This time, the address given was right across the street from his house. The other officer checking on the call up the road answered up on the radio and said, "That's impossible. I'm literally in front of that residence right now, and no one has crossed the road." With all the calls coming in and beginning to pile up, the young officer told the man that he would return to finish taking his statement and that he was going to help the other officer canvas the neighborhood in search of this girl.

A short time later, the officer returned. "I just don't understand it," he said. We received several more calls from different residents about that girl, each time the same story. She knocks, asks for help, and then she disappears. There was absolutely no way she could've kept crossing the road and avoiding us as we were searching. He told the man that since he was the first to report the call, he would use his version and add the rest of the reports to the one call. "I guess some things you just can't explain," the officer said as he bid the man goodnight and walked down the driveway, now with a trace of snow on it, to his patrol car.

The man's wife went back upstairs to bed, and he told her that he would be up directly. He sat down in a chair in the den in the darkness. Outside he watched as the snow continued to fall, heavier now illuminated by the streetlight out front. As he sat, he pondered the events of the evening. "What could it have been? Was it really a girl in trouble, or had he quite possibly had an encounter with a ghost?" Though all his years of education screamed for a logical, practical answer, he could never reconcile to himself that there was one. Perhaps the answer to his question was best summed up by the young officer that night. "I guess some things you just can't explain."

Strange Happenings in the Kress Building

The Kress Building

Durham has many old buildings downtown, most associated with its early tobacco manufacturing history. One of the most exciting and unique buildings architecturally is the structure located on Main Street that once housed the S.H. Kress Company store. The business, founded by Samuel Kress as a 5,10, or 25 cent store in 1896, was located all across the country. This particular building was built between 1932 and 1933, and it stands as a rare example of Art Deco style in North Carolina. The building is richly decorated with terracotta ornaments of Aztec and Mayan design. The richly decorated interior still retains many of its Art Deco fixtures, including the high ceilings, crown moldings, light fixtures, and elevator doors. The one in Durham has remained true to the architect's original visionary ideals. Today, the building has been uniquely preserved, containing modern condo units and commercial spaces. But at night, when the lights are low and foot traffic is minimal, do the spirits of the past walk the historical structure? Strangely, there have been reports of haunts that go back to its earliest days when it was reasonably new construction.

During World War II, Durham was a busy hub on the liberty circuit for soldiers stationed north of the city at Camp Butner. Saturdays and Sundays would find the weary soldiers on a weekend pass coming in and out of the store; most of them would sit at the lunch counter to order food that was, if nothing else, a brief relief from Army chow. Many of them just wanted a short escape into the civilian world again for a few moments before returning to the base and eventually the battlefields in Europe, Africa, and Asia.

During this busy time, a young teenage girl worked at the lunch counter as a waitress. She was used to the soldiers coming in, flirting, and laughing. She went along with them, knowing that most were far from home, and she wanted to make them as comfortable as she could while they were there. The lunch counter would be so lively, and the hustle and bustle would keep the girl busy until the last customer left, and it was time to clean up. If she were the last one there for cleanup, she would always try to get a manager to stay with her as she cleaned. No matter what, she still felt as though she was being watched and as if someone were standing directly over her shoulder.

The feeling was so real that many nights she would turn out the lights when done and run from the lunchroom, not looking back. The young girl continued to work the counter for several years but would always describe the nights she closed as terrifying. Though she could never put her finger on precisely what it was, she would remember the feelings she had when alone in that lunchroom for the rest of her life.

Similarly, there is another story during that same time frame involving another young girl. This young girl had a frightening experience when she heard someone calling her name as she entered a storeroom to retrieve supplies. The girl momentarily stopped to listen as she heard her name, but the silence quickly forced her to resume her mission of gathering the supplies. Suddenly the door slammed shut, and with no one around, she was trapped, and her cries for help went unheard. She was found hours later sweating profusely and crying, desperately trying to claw her way out. Her reportedly cruel and demanding father had recently passed, and she believed that it was his spirit terrorizing her.

Could these hauntings be related? Could the ghost of the girl's deceased father be the same spirit that terrorized his daughter and be the terrifying experience that hovered over the scared figure of the other young female employee that spent so many miserable nights closing? We will never know for sure, but it does make one wonder if, among the businesses and condos today, that same entity moves among the living, unseen and waiting once more for the right moment to make its presence known and felt.

Ghosts of Stagville

The Stagville Plantation House

In the beautiful rolling hills of northern Durham County stands Stagville Plantation, today a North Carolina State Historic site. Stagville was once one of the most extensive plantations in the south, encompassing thousands of acres of land and hundreds of slaves owned by Richard Bennehan.

Bennehan came to North Carolina from Petersburg, Virginia, where he had served as an apprentice storekeeper. In 1768, he purchased an interest in the store of William Johnston of Snow Hill Plantation, which was part of Orange County. Becoming very successful, he built the one and a half story structure at Stagville in 1787, followed in

1799 by the two-story Georgian style addition to the home. The completed stately design served as the seat of his 4,000-acre plantation.

Richard Bennehan was a well-respected citizen and merchant in the community. In 1792, he served as a member of the building committee for the new state capital in Raleigh, and after 1799, he was a trustee of the state university at Chapel Hill. The family was a happy one and for years prospered in the region. The Bennehans were blessed with two children, a son Thomas and a daughter Rebecca. Rebecca married Duncan Cameron and settled on nearby Fairntosh Plantation, which was deeded to them by her father as a wedding gift. In 1825 at Richard Bennehan's death, Stagville passed to his son Thomas. Sadly, Thomas, a lifelong bachelor, passed in 1847, and Stagville became part of Fairntosh Plantation. Today there is a beautiful and large cut stone-walled cemetery within yards of the house. Sadly, the large lot contains three lone individuals Richard, his wife, and son Thomas. It is a testament to one man's dream of a sizeable dynastic family that was not to be.

Further to the north of the main plantation house stands Horton Grove, a slave quarters complex for the estate. On this tract is a story and a half house with a chimney. This late 18th-century log home is believed to be the home of Mr. Horton, from whom Richard purchased the property. This home, in later years, probably served as the house of the plantation's overseer. The two-story slave houses located there were built after Thomas acquired the land from his father in 1825. Untypical of many slave dwellings, the two-story apartment-style homes each had four rooms, two downstairs and two upstairs with four families housed in each building, with one room with a large fireplace for cooking and heating per family.

It is no wonder there are so many strange reports in these two locations' activities with such an old and deep history. In the main house, many employees over the years have reported cold spots, even in the hot summer months. Many items are said to be moved from where they were placed by staff. This often occurs even though alarms are armed and doors are locked overnight. Occasionally, the interior motion detectors are set off late at night and early in the morning. When authorities arrive, no one is present, and the doors and windows are secured with nothing having been disturbed.

Horton Grove Slave House

One deputy reported after checking on the plantation late one evening that as he cleared the call and drove away, a mysterious knocking could be heard on the protective cage from the back seat of his car. It was as if someone were knocking on the glass right beside his head. This so unnerved the deputy that he quickly made his way to the lights of town. He grabbed a cup of coffee to calm his nerves, having been convinced that he had given a ride to a ghostly hitchhiker from the old plantation. To this day, he remains cautious not to venture near Stagville at night once it has been closed to visitors unless it was necessary. Convinced he has already given a ride to one phantom hitchhiker, he has no desire to pick up another.

18th Century Horton House

Not to be outdone by the main house's spirits, Horton Grove's ghosts are just as restless. Reports of a young black girl wandering the grounds have been reported, and at first, she is not immediately recognized as a ghost. Those who see her are often convinced she is a lost child and report the sighting only to find that there have been no missing children reported. Occasionally, fire alarms will be reported at the old barn near the slave quarters, but the Fire Department responds only to discover that there is no fire or any fire signs present.

The home and grounds stand empty now, a museum to the past. The spirits of those many people who lived on this property, white and black, will be ever-present watching over and looking after the home they held so dear so many years ago.

Old Barn

A Visit from Rosa

In the early days of the Erwin Cotton Mill, West Durham was a distinct community with its own identity. It had its shops, schools, and recreational facilities. Everyone knew everyone and everyone, for the most part, worked at the mill. For one family that lived on Dezern Place near Hale Street, warm summer evening events would bewilder and amaze them for years to come.

That day had been a hot one, and most of the family had worked the first shift at the mill. They had got off work in the afternoon while their daughter, who had a small child, was headed in for the second shift leaving her little boy with her parents to watch until she would get off late that night. Typical of families at that time, they took their supper then headed out to the front porch to enjoy the cool of the evening before bedtime.

On this evening, as they sat talking and laughing, the family's father looked up to see his daughter Rosa coming down the street. They all thought she was coming home to grab a quick bite to eat and then run back to work. As she neared the front of the house, she kept right on walking, never looking up as she passed.

Her father stood up and called "Rosa, Rosa," but she kept right on walking past the house.

The father stepped off the porch and into the street, but she was already gone. For the life of them, they could not figure out why she would walk past them without even acknowledging their existence and how she could have disappeared so quickly. Later that night, when she came home from work, the family waited up for her and confronted her to know why she had acted so strangely earlier. Rosa swore to the family that she had never left work that night and nervously laughed it off, telling her mother, father, and siblings that they must have been seeing things.

For her family, it was strange, strange indeed, for it was less than two weeks later that they stood in the rain under a large oak tree in the cemetery and watched as they lowered Rosa into the ground while comforting her small son. Did Rosa somehow know that her time was near, for it was right after her vision was seen that she fell sick? Was her spirit beginning to prematurely wander away from her earthly state to her celestial home? This is what her family thought, and they never forgot that night for as long as they lived.

Haunted Duke University and Hospital

Duke University's origins can be traced back to 1838 when what was to become Trinity College opened in Randolph County. The school would see several name changes in its early years before finally settling on Trinity in 1859. Within three decades of that last name change, Trinity College would move to Durham's bustling new town through Washington Duke and Julian Carr's philanthropic efforts. The new campus would be settled on the old racetrack west of the city, occupying East Campus's present location.

In 1924 with the establishment of the Duke Endowment by James B. Duke, money was generously distributed throughout the Carolinas, funding hospitals, orphanages, and the Methodist Church. This endowment's large benefactor was Trinity College, with three colleges and a university added to the growing complex. This generous donation was rewarded when President William Few of Trinity insisted that the university be named Duke University in honor of the family.

With the East Campus off and running, construction began on the West Campus, and by 1930 most of the beautiful Gothic Revival buildings were opened along with the hospital and medical school. The landmark chapel was completed in

1935, making Duke University a sprawling state-of-the-art campus.

There is a dark side, however, to this lovely and serene environment. Ghosts have reportedly been seen on all areas of the campus, both east and west. Sightings have ranged from spectral figures seen in Wallace Wade Stadium's stands to sounds of echoes and laughter throughout the Ark on East Campus. The old gymnasium was built from salvaged lumber from the old racetrack grandstands. Could these be the disembodied voices of fans from the early days at the old racetrack? Or, could it be the laughter of students in the ancient gymnasium from days gone by? Perhaps it is a mixture of both.

Located near the West Campus, the hospital has seen its share of emotional energy over the years. Like all hospitals, supernatural events seem to be expected, and Duke Hospital is no exception. Built-in 1930, it is one of the most renowned medical centers in the world. Every year thousands of people move through this bustling environment, each with their own stories of pain and emotion. With all the activity and emotional energy, there is no wonder the hospital is a hotbed of paranormal activity.

Elevators are known to move up and down the shaft as if summoned by some unseen hand that travels from floor-to-floor void of occupants. One former campus police officer reported that late one night, he received a call. He had been requested to escort a nurse to pick up supplies from a desolate storage area in the hospital. Thinking that the nurses were afraid of the site because of possible intruders in the building due to the room's remoteness, he willingly followed along. Surprisingly to the officer, he was instead inundated with stories about ghosts from the nurse as they made their way down the hall, and she spoke only of how frightened she was to be alone.

As the officer stood silently listening to her stories, he propped the door to the storage room where she was now working with a wedge that he had found on the floor. Finally, after hearing enough of the stories, the officer laughed at her and then scoffed at her foolishness for believing in such things. At that very moment, the door slammed into the back of the officer with such force that it almost knocked him off his feet. He thought for sure that someone had been inside the room hiding behind the door and had forcefully pushed the door into him. Regaining his composure, he quickly inspected the room and found no one was present aside from himself and the nurse, no one visible at least. The wedge that had been holding the door open had been rocketed halfway down the hall. The two quickly finished their task and returned to the more populated area of the hospital. The officer to this very day swears that only some inhuman force could have moved that door so violently that night, and from thenceforth, he was not so quick to reject the ghost stories that were told about the hospital.

Duke University and its hospital operate daily with thousands of people's activity, and the beautiful old structures by day are graceful and reserved. Still, one cannot say that those same old buildings at night don't assume a different aura. Nights on the campus can be reminiscent of gothic castles and can conjure up images from Victorian ghost stories as shadows are cast amongst these imposing structures. It is no wonder with such a rich and full history that there are those from the past that still walk among these grand old buildings with the living. If you are there and look very carefully, you may be lucky enough to catch a glimpse of one of those apparitions from long ago.

Trinity College-Duke East Campus

Restless Spirits of Cabe Cemetery

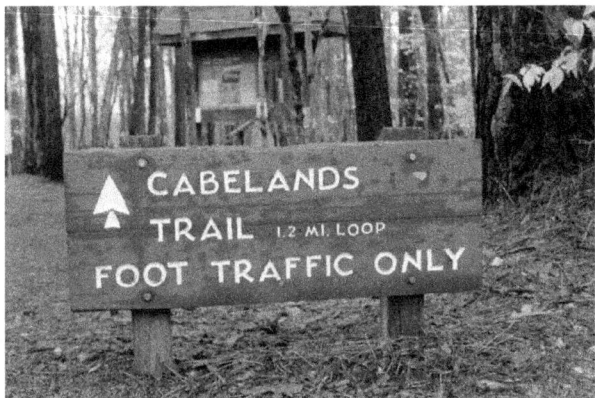

Cabelands Trail sign

West of Durham off Sparger Road is the Cabe Lands Trail. Located along the meandering Eno River and part of the North Carolina State Parks System, the trails are a peaceful and serene environment. They often serve as a welcome escape from the busy city. The area is perfect for a day outing to get away and clear one's mind from the hustle and bustle of daily life. But beware, locked inside this peaceful atmosphere, things tend to change quickly, almost at a moment's notice, especially when it begins to get dark in and around the old Cabe Family Cemetery.

This area was one of the earliest areas to be settled in modern-day Durham County. As the site grew, mills sprang up along the Flat and Eno

Rivers, and many of these families would become some of Durham's early elites. One of these families was the Cabe family. Squire John Cabe, the patriarch, owned a mill along the Eno and several others in the region. Over the years, the squire had three wives that gave him nine daughters whom he cherished. As he had no son to continue his legacy, he ensured that his daughters were well cared for. Through marriage, they would become entwined with other prosperous families in the region, such as the McCowns, another thriving mill owning family.

They wanted to keep his family as close in death as in life. Squire John established the Cabe Family Cemetery. The cemetery is surrounded by large, majestic hardwoods, providing a canopy from the sun, and often casting eerie shadows amongst the rows of tombstones, including old Squire John and other members of the Cabe and McCown family. Though it appears serene, a feeling of uneasiness often pervades the environment in and around the cemetery. Reports of children crying and sometimes laughing cause an unsettling of nerves amongst wary visitors.

Many who have ventured into the area, especially around dusk, often claim to have what they describe as an emotionally draining experience, and many refuse to return. Most of the activity in the cemetery is usually around a large granite stone. The stone is the final resting placed of Moses Ellis McCown, an early mayor of

Durham. People report extreme cold spots around the stone, even during the hottest days of summer. The areas may move but usually stay within proximity to the rock. Several years ago, two men visiting the site in search of the cold spots they had heard so much about were not disappointed. The two discovered the cold spots near the stone precisely as they had heard. Even though it was a warm spring day, they could insert their hands into the cold pocket of air, the cold pocket would move periodically, but the drastic temperature difference would remain the same no matter where it would move.

Not only in the cemetery but the area surrounding it also has a different feel about it. Some have described it as a feeling that you should not be there. A possible reason for this is what occurred in the area in the winter of 1971. One late February afternoon, a surveyor working on a job in the Cabe Lands area off Sparger Road got out of his truck to gather his tools. As he looked over into the woods, he saw what appeared to be a mannequin's leg sticking out from behind a tree. To his horror, as he approached, he saw the bodies of a man and a woman slumped over one another, leaning against a tree. Their hands had been tied behind their backs, and leaves and branches partially covered their bodies, victims of a possible brutal fit of jealousy that erupted sometime after they were last seen on Valentine's night. Adding to the mystery, this gruesome murder has never been solved.

Are these feelings and experiences of so many people just a figment of their imaginations? Or if there are spirits present, why are they so restless? Could it be the spirit of the two lovers seeking justice to the wrong done to them in life, or could it be a member of the Cabe or McCown family that can't peacefully move on? Maybe something was left undone. No matter the answer to these questions, it's entirely possible that as the sun begins to go down and day turns to dusk, we should leave these restless spirits to their wooded abode.

Cabe Cemetery gravestones

The Ghost Upstairs

An apartment complex seems a relatively rare place to find a ghost, but one such building in Durham houses at least one. The old Palm Park Apartment building was built in the 1960s and, at its time, was one of the finest apartment complexes around; which was noted for its style and modernity, it was considered a premium location to live. Young families or on-the-go singles moved in and out of the apartments throughout the years. Most of them lived there a while then moved on, but it seems that some of them stayed behind.

One night in the 1980s, two boys crossed paths with a former resident. The boys were very close, and they would spend many of their summer evenings spending the night at each other's house, and as most boys do, they would stay up late into the evening playing and at times being a bit loud and raucous.

One of the boys lived in an apartment at Palm Park with his mother. As usual, the other boy was spending the weekend with them; their day had already been spent playing and swimming at the nearby pool. It was now dark, and both boys had been confined to the prison of being locked inside the rest of the night. This was the most miserable time for both, for upstairs there lived an elderly widow. Anytime they made the slightest bit of noise, she would bang on the floor with her broom, letting them know she was upstairs, and they had best quiet down.

The boy's mother always cautioned them to calm down as the woman had already caused her a considerable amount of trouble by complaining about her. One evening, the boys and the mother were in the living room watching a movie when they noticed red lights flashing inside the apartment. They all got up and looked out of the window to see an ambulance out front. The mother told the two boys to stay inside as she went out to find out what was going on. She returned a few moments later and said to them that the elderly widow who lived upstairs had passed away.

Later that night, the boys finished watching a movie and became restless and began playing, getting a little out of control. The mother came in and quieted them, telling them to keep the noise down. At that point, the boy staying with them joked that it was ok now since the woman was no longer there, and with that, they all started laughing as the boys began jokingly running around and purposely acting up. It was then that they heard it ever so slight, they all stopped what they were doing and listened, and there it was again, the unmistakable pounding on the floor from the empty apartment above. Bewildered, they looked at each other while in their minds searching for some rational explanation for what had just happened.

Thinking that someone, a family member, maybe had come back to the apartment, they all ran outside. The boys crept out of the front door and looked up at the window and the door where the old lady used to live. Upstairs there were no lights on, just a stillness and a deathly silence. Everything was unearthly quiet. Is it possible that the spirit of the widow was still inside her home? Is it possible she didn't realize that her physical body had passed earlier, and her energy had remained behind? Hopefully, the woman has found the peace and quiet in death that she sought in life.

Haunted House on Hawthorne Drive

On the western outskirts of the city limits, there stands a home on Hawthorne Drive that looks just a little different from the rest of them surrounding it. The house sits at an odd angle and further back from the road. When the neighborhood was built in the 1940s, the original part of the home was already in existence, according to two elderly sisters that grew up in the area.

During the neighborhood construction, two bedrooms and a bathroom were added to the older structure already on the lot. The chimney used to be at the end of the house, as it was facing a different direction from the newer homes, was now in the front of the house with a new door added to make it face in a uniform direction.

In the early 1960s, the home was purchased by a young couple. Shortly after they moved in, they were approached by a lady well into her 80's they guessed. She told them that she used to play in the original part of their house as a child. She told the couple that the house was old and abandoned even then in the late 1800s. She said to them that back in those days, the home sat way back off the road, which she referred to as an old pig path when the neighborhood was nothing but forests and fields.

From the time they moved in, they noticed strange things. The husband would hear strange noises in the night, sounds like someone's heavy footsteps walking back and forth in the house's original part. He kept things mostly to himself to keep from frightening his family. He did not want anything to disrupt the peace in their new home, and they were to spend many happy years together there raising their two sons.

Though the husband tried to keep things quiet, the unexplained happenings continued over the years, and after their sons grew up and moved from home, the activity seemed to increase. Things became so frequent that the wife was now noticing strange things. Now not only did they hear footsteps, but they were beginning to hear voices. The voices would be loud and frequent as if someone were trying to talk in a loud whisper, but the words were not discernable.

One night while the husband watched television in the living room, one of the two old original rooms, he gasped and called for his wife. As she entered the room, his gaze was fixated in the corner. There she watched as a white mist began forming. As it fully developed into a thick shapeless blob, it began to move across the room, and just as quickly as it appeared, it was gone, leaving the couple staring in disbelief at what they had just witnessed.

The years have passed by quickly. The husband has since passed away, but the wife still lives in the home. After almost 60 years there, she has come to accept whatever it is that resides in the home with her. She always tries to tell herself that there is a logical explanation, creaking floorboards, or just an old house settling. Still, deep down, she knows the truth, for she has witnessed it many times with her own eyes, and so she remains content to cohabitate with whomever from the past still lingers in the home with her.

The Catsburg Ghost Train

It had been a tranquil evening, with only a couple of breaking and entering calls and one traffic accident. All the calls had come out early in the shift, and the lack of them had made the hours drag by as the young man shifted uncomfortably in his seat. He had been a deputy sheriff for about a year, and he was still trying to acclimate his body to working those long overnight shifts.

It was late fall, and the air was cold and crisp outside as he sat in the warmth of his patrol car parked behind the old Catsburg store. He had caught himself dozing off a couple of times already, and he rolled down his window to let in the cool night air. There was nothing but silence outside. The store was closed, and only an occasional car would pass by going down Old Oxford Highway.

The cool air felt good on his face, and he decided to get out of his car and walk around awhile to keep himself awake. He looked at the back of the old store as he walked around the gravel lot that was starting to grow up. He looked up at the dilapidated boards beginning to rot and thought about what a thriving store must have been in earlier times. He thought about the name Catsburg, named after a former sheriff of Durham County, "Cat Belvin." He had earned that nickname by being able to sneak up on and catch moonshiners during the prohibition era and after.

As he kicked an old, weathered baseball lying in the parking lot by the ball field was when he first heard it. It was faint at first, so quiet that he hardly even noticed it; if it had not been for the dead stillness of the night around him, he probably would not have even heard it at all. Then it came again, this time a little bit louder; it was the sound of a far-off train. As he stood there motionless in the cold night, the unmistakable sound of the train moved closer and closer. He could hear the whistle blow, and he knew that it was coming from the tracks beside the old store. There was just one problem: the tracks behind the store had not been in use for years.

He could now feel the rumble of the approaching train under his feet, and the light on the engine was now visible, casting an eerie glow through the trees as it made its approach. The haunting sound of the whistle blew once more as the deputy stood staring in disbelief. Then as suddenly as it had appeared, it was gone. There was nothing, no sound, no light, no reverberations and rumbling of the passing cars on the old rusty tracks, just stillness. It was gone, and back was the dark silent night.

The confused deputy made his way back to his vehicle and collapsed in the seat. He needed to get his mind wrapped around what had just occurred. He sat staring once again at the old store and looked in his rear-view mirror in the darkness towards Hamlin Road where the old tracks used to cross. He tried to convince himself that what happened was impossible; there is no way that a train can appear and disappear out of nothing but thin air, but it had, he had witnessed it. As the night slowly dragged on, he pulled his car out of the gravel lot onto the road questioning his sanity, but as he drove off that night, one thing became very apparent. He was sure that there are just some things that we will never understand and some things in this world that are just best left alone.

For years, the tracks around the old Catsburg Store have had many reports of spectral encounters. Tales of a man killed one-night years ago on the tracks by an oncoming train have led to sightings of a shadowy headless form of a man walking the tracks in the darkness. Reports of a mysterious light filtering through the trees along the tracks and the sound of a train whistle can be heard echoing through the night. The old store is now gone, and traffic has significantly increased over the years with the extension of Carver Street to Old Oxford Highway. Will the Catsburg ghost train maintain its ghostly run with this increase in traffic and development? Only time will tell.

The tracks at Catsburg

Angel Music

During the 1920s, factories dominated Durham, and many of the residents found themselves living in mill houses all over town. One such couple lived in one of those homes in the West Durham Erwin Cotton Mill village. Those were good days for the young family. Their union had already been blessed with a son's birth, soon followed by the birth of a baby girl. The couple worked hard and took great care to provide for their children. When the baby girl was about six months old, she took ill; the mother worried over her daughter and watched over her night and day. A doctor was summoned, but he did not feel that it was anything seriously wrong with the child and reassured the parents that there was nothing to worry about. The mother continued to take care of the home, watching over the family and taking care of the day-to-day tasks of running the house while the father would labor all day in the mill.

One night, the exhausted mother, having sat up with the baby for hours, decided that she had to get some rest. As she laid down, sleep quickly overtook her, and she was soon in a deep sleep. As she lay there in bed, she was quickly awakened by what she described as the most beautiful strains of music that she had ever heard. She sat up in bed and listened for a moment. She looked down at her sleeping husband and called his name, but he did not stir. She got out of her bed and put on her housecoat. She opened the windows to listen, but the night was dead still, and she heard nothing coming from outside, but as soon as she pulled her head back inside, she heard the music again. She could not describe the tune or even the instrument playing it, but she knew it was beautiful. The mother decided that since she was awake, she would go and check on her little daughter. As she entered the room, the music suddenly stopped; she looked down into the crib and discovered that her precious child had passed away during the night.

The grief-stricken woman and her husband buried their baby girl in the churchyard beside other family members. The mother who would live to be in her 80's would swear for the rest of her life that the beautiful music she heard that night was angels coming to take her sweet little child to heaven.

The Crying at the Bridge

By the early 1920s, Durham was a bustling textile town; to say the least, it was probably in its heyday. Tall buildings, streetcars, movie theatres filled downtown, motor cars raced down paved streets, and electric lights lit up the night sky. This was not so for the county; for the most part, one could not tell they were even in the twentieth century. Dirt roads and paths led through small communities, and many people were still getting around on horseback or in wagons, and it was miles of wilderness with no electricity or streetlight to light the way.

Such was the world a young farmer that lived in the Little River area of North Durham was accustomed to. Just a few years before, the young man had been a soldier in the trenches in France fighting back the Hun. Fortunately, and by God's grace, he had made it back home. He had saved a little money from his time in the army, and with work he had been doing at odd jobs, he had at last put aside a good deal of money, and he was able to put down a hefty down payment on a small farm in the area. Not only was he purchasing a farm, but he had also met a nice young lady at church who lived just a couple of miles away that he had set his eyes on. His life was going wonderfully, and he began courting the young lady and visiting with her in the late summer afternoons. The two would spend hours on the front porch talking about their future together and getting married. After supper, they would take long evening strolls and enjoy the beauty of the countryside. At the end of his visits, the young man would bid the family farewell and travel a couple of miles back to his own family's farm on an old mule that he owned. His mind would be full of dreams of marriage, starting a family, and building a house on the piece of land he had just purchased. He usually crested the top of the ridge by his home just as the sun would be waning through the trees in the western sky.

Now the leaves were beginning to change, and the long days of summer were shortened into the shorter days of early fall. No one enjoyed traveling through the dark paths at night in those days, but love has a strange way of making people do things they do not necessarily want to do, and he wasn't about to cut short his Sunday dinners and courting time at the young lady's home. The young man was not afraid anyhow; he had witnessed firsthand the horrors of trench warfare in France during the Great War. Besides, his mind was usually occupied the entire way home with his fantasies and dreams of what he hoped was just around the corner for him and his soon-to-be bride.

One incredibly inky black night, as he made his way home, his mind was wandering as usual as he rounded the bend headed for an old creek crossing, he heard a noise. At first, it sounded way off in the distance, but it became louder and louder. It sounded as if a small child was crying, and it was coming from near the old footbridge that spanned the creek. The closer he got to the bridge, the louder the crying sound became; he called out, but there was no answer. He strained his eyes, trying to see in the dark; by the light of a sliver moon, he could make out the outline of the old footbridge but could see no one walking about.

He moved closer to the bridge, his mind now moving in a million directions. Gone were the beautiful daydreams of a few minutes before his mind was now filled with every ghost, booger, witch, and haunting story he had ever been told, and it was with much trepidation that he slid off the back of the old mule to get a closer look. As he inched closer and closer to the old bridge, he called out, but nothing answered. He moved a few feet closer, strained his eyes in the darkness, and called out once more.

Suddenly a piercing cry broke through the night and echoed through the dark bottoms, and what he would later describe as the largest bobcat he had ever seen in his life bounded from underneath the bridge and took off into the darkness. So frightened was the mule that he instantly ran off with the young farmer still holding the reigns and the saddle. Luckily, hanging onto the side of the animal, he could get one leg over the top of the old mule, but there was no slowing him down. Hanging on for dear life, he bounded through the forest.

The young man was being beaten half to death with tree branches, limbs, and briars all the way home. Exhausted from his adventure, it was a weary man that slid off the mule. He lay on the ground as the mule walked himself to the barn that night. He lay there for several minutes before he could muster the strength to trudge inside and collapse exhausted in his bed. That frightening occurrence would be a story that he told for the rest of his life, many times around the stove of an old country store with his intent listeners laughing hysterically at the playful way he regaled his tale.

Yes, he did marry the young lady, and they did build a home on that piece of land he had purchased. They lived happily on that land for many years and raised many children. Over the years, through children, grandchildren, and great-grandchildren, the story grew and grew each time he told it. By the time the old farmer passed away, the bobcat had grown to the size of a Bengal Tiger. Very few today remember the tale from the older man, as he passed away years ago, but his legend lives on to those who knew him and those who had the privilege of hearing him recount this great adventure.

The Bull Woman

This story takes place in the old Hickstown area of Durham in the 1920s and '30s. At that time, the bus service was in its infancy and was run by Duke Power Company. In those days, the last bus stop in West Durham was in the old West Durham Lumber Company on Hillsborough Road.

Uncle Joe was an older man born years before in Orange County. He had been born with a veil over his face, a thin layer of skin said by the old-timers to give the individual born with it "special sight." In the early 1890s, with the Erwin Cotton Mill opening, most of his family moved into Durham to work in the mill. He would often walk from the area of what is now Pleasant Green Road in Orange County to visit with his relatives. In his later years, he would be seen walking along the old Hillsborough Road in an old army trench coat, making the long trek home from Durham.

When the buses started to run, Uncle Joe would often, if he stayed later than expected, catch the bus to its last stop to save a mile or two on his old, tired feet. Many nights on the last bus run, the streets at the edge of town would be dark and empty. As he would exit the bus onto the dark lonely street, he would be greeted by what he described as the "Bull Woman." According to him, there would be a lady in a long dress and bonnet sitting side-saddle on a bull. Concerned, he would always speak to her and ask her why she was out so late and what she was doing sitting side straddle on a bull. Every time she would stare intently at him and then slowly ride off, vanishing in the darkness. Over the years, Uncle Joe saw the Bull Woman many times, and after all of those encounters, he never received an answer to any of the questions presented to her.

Uncle Joe has been dead for many years now, but he always enjoyed telling people the Bull Woman story. He said it was most appropriate that the Bull City should have a Bull Woman that rides the night on the back of a bull. Throughout the year's thanks to Uncle Joe, more than one West Durham child was told to get in before the sun goes down or the Bull Woman will get you.

The Durham Bull

About the Author

William Jackson is a local author and amateur historian that resides in Durham with his wife and children. A graduate of Campbell University and a native of Durham, he has spent years gathering folktales and history from the surrounding area.

Did You Enjoy Bull City Ghosts?

I hope that you have enjoyed purchasing and reading Bull City Ghosts! If you have enjoyed the book I would love for you to take a moment to review the book on Amazon. Your feedback allows me to make improvements to my books as well as guide me to new and interesting topics that I can write about in the future.

Other Books by William Jackson

Ghosts of the Triangle: Historic Haunts of Raleigh, Durham, and Chapel Hill

Family Ghosts: The Jackson Family Haunting